PICTURE LIBRARY

CROCODILES
AND
ALLIGATORS

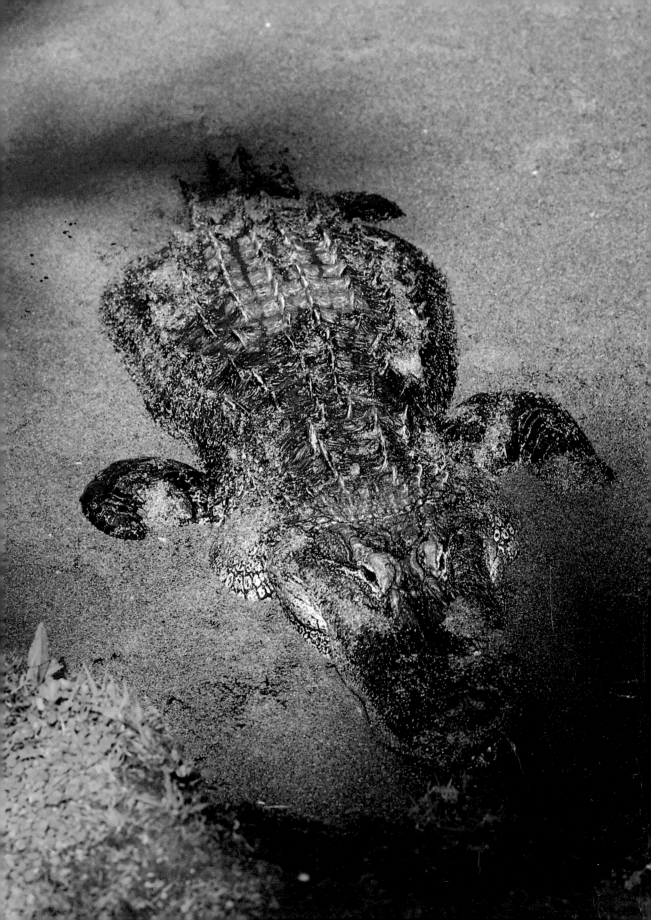

PICTURE LIBRARY

CROCODILES
AND
ALLIGATORS

Norman Barr

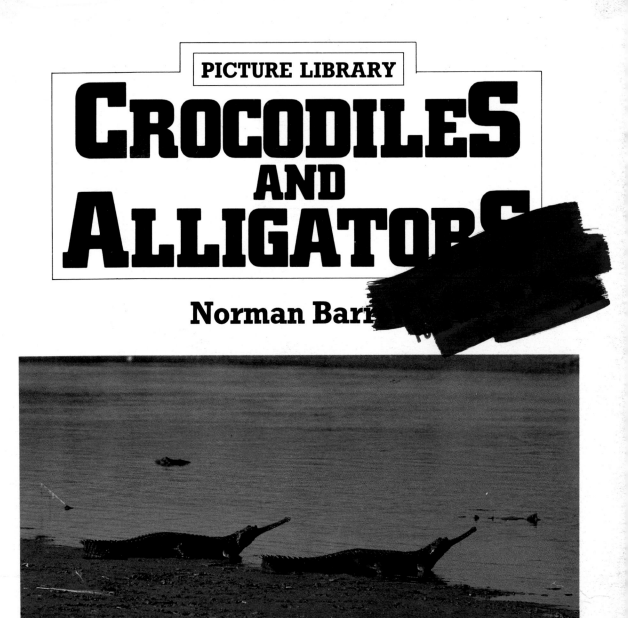

Franklin Watts

London   New York   Sydney   Toronto

© 1989 Franklin Watts Ltd

First published in Great Britain
  1989 by
Franklin Watts Ltd
12a Golden Square
London W1R 4BA

First published in the USA by
Franklin Watts Inc
387 Park Avenue South
New York
NY 10016

First published in Australia by
Franklin Watts
14 Mars Road
Lane Cove
NSW 2066

UK ISBN: 0 86313 816 0
US ISBN: 0-531-10705 1
Library of Congress Catalog Card
Number 88–51517

Printed in Italy

Designed by
Barrett & Weintroub

Photographs by
Survival Anglia
N.S. Barrett
Pat Morris

Illustration by
Rhoda & Robert Burns

Technical Consultant
Michael Chinery

Contents

Introduction

Crocodiles and alligators are among the largest reptiles on earth. They are the survivors of a group of giant prehistoric reptiles that included the dinosaurs.

Together with caimans and the gharial, crocodiles and alligators belong to an order in the animal kingdom called crocodilians. They have armored skins, long snouts and sharp cone-shaped teeth.

△ The fearsome looking jaws and teeth of a Nile crocodile. Lying with its mouth open helps a crocodile to cool down.

Crocodilians are found in most of the tropical parts of the world. They live mainly in shallow water, slow-moving rivers and swamps.

They use their tail to propel themselves through the water, and have webbed feet that enable them to move fast on soft ground.

Crocodilians eat most things that they can catch – fish, frogs, birds and small mammals. They sometimes attack large animals and people.

△ American alligators basking in the sun of the Everglades, in Florida. They like to soak up the warmth during the day and hunt for food at night.

Looking at crocodilians

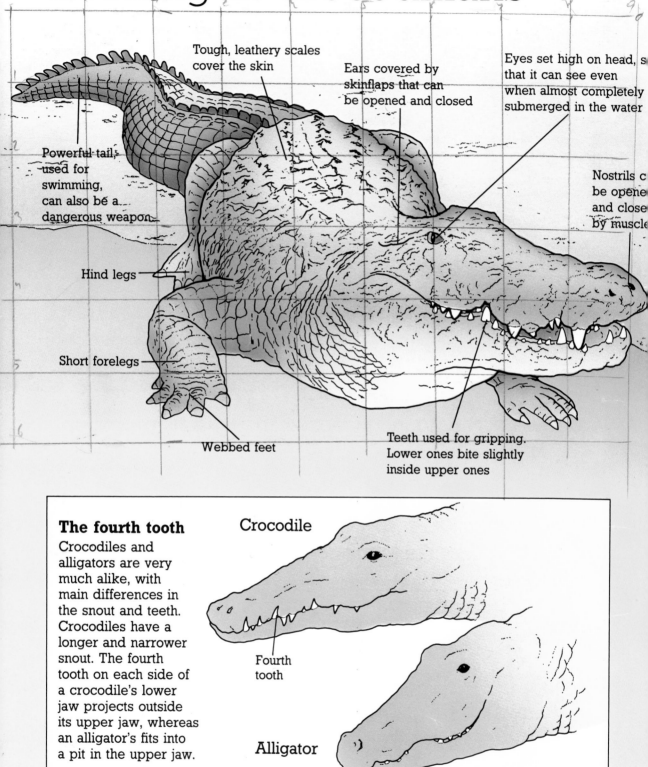

Tough, leathery scales cover the skin

Ears covered by skinflaps that can be opened and closed

Eyes set high on head, s that it can see even when almost completely submerged in the water

Powerful tail, used for swimming, can also be a dangerous weapon

Nostrils c be opene and close by muscle

Hind legs

Short forelegs

Webbed feet

Teeth used for gripping. Lower ones bite slightly inside upper ones

The fourth tooth

Crocodiles and alligators are very much alike, with main differences in the snout and teeth. Crocodiles have a longer and narrower snout. The fourth tooth on each side of a crocodile's lower jaw projects outside its upper jaw, whereas an alligator's fits into a pit in the upper jaw.

Crocodile

Fourth tooth

Alligator

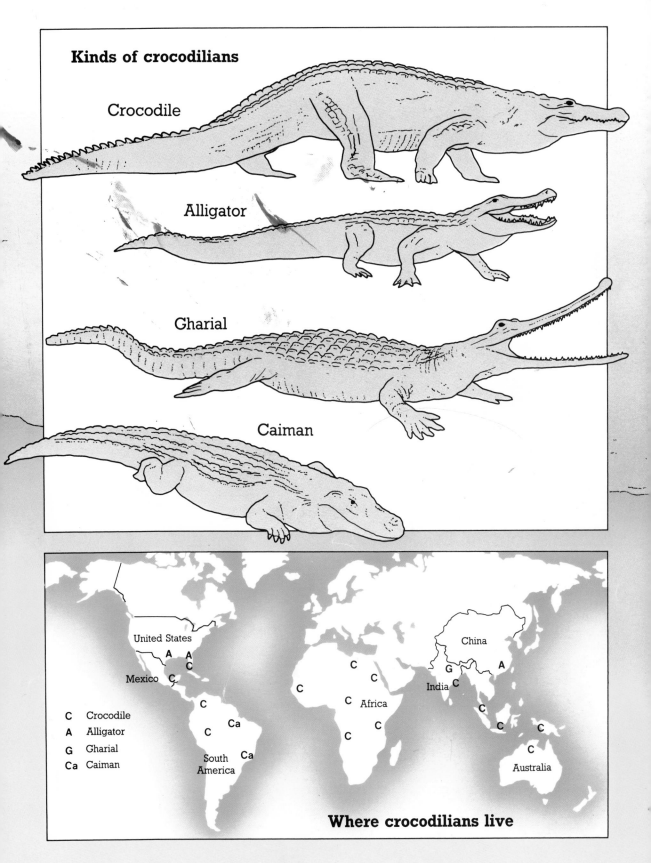

Kinds of crocodilians

Crocodile

Alligator

Gharial

Caiman

C Crocodile
A Alligator
G Gharial
Ca Caiman

United States

Mexico

South
America

Africa

India

China

Australia

Where crocodilians live

Kinds of crocodilians

Although crocodiles and alligators have different names, they are very much alike. There are only minor differences.

There are more than a dozen species (kinds) of crocodiles. They are found in the Americas, Africa, Asia and Australia. There are two species of alligator, the American and the Chinese. The caimans, sometimes called alligators, live in Central and South America. The gharial lives in northern India.

△ The American alligator has a broad snout. American alligators are generally smaller than their crocodile cousins, averaging 2.5–3 m (8–10 ft) in length.

▷ The Nile crocodile is found in most parts of Africa except the Sahara region and the northern coast.

▽ The American crocodile is found in southern Florida, Central America and the Caribbean. Most kinds of crocodiles have more pointed snouts than alligators. Crocodiles average about 3.7 m (12 ft) in length, although specimens nearly twice that size have been found.

△ The estuarine, or saltwater, crocodile thrives in river mouths and sea water. It is found on the east coast of India, Indonesia and Australia. The largest of the crocodilians, it attacks large animals and is very dangerous to human beings.

▷ The marsh crocodile, or "mugger," is found in inland waters of India and Sri Lanka. It rarely attacks people.

▷ The Siamese crocodile has been found in Java and in the rivers of south east Asia.

▷ The gharial is easy to tell apart from other crocodilians because of its long, slender snout, which it uses to catch fish with a sideways snap. The gharial lives in northern India and is one of the largest crocodilians.

▷ A dwarf caiman resting with its head above the water. The dwarf caiman is one of the smallest of the crocodilians, reaching at most 1.2 m (4 ft). Other caimans are two or three times as large. Dwarf caimans live in swift, rocky rivers.

On land and in water

Crocodilians are at home both in and out of the water. With eyes and nostrils on top of the head, they can see and breathe when almost completely submerged in water.

They open and close their nostrils with special muscles that prevent water getting in when they dive. They can also shut off their windpipes from the rest of their mouth. This enables them to open their jaws without inhaling water.

△ An alligator swims through the water, almost submerged. Its eyes and nostrils are just above the water surface.

Most crocodilians are fast swimmers, using their powerful tails to speed through the water. For paddling slowly, they use their feet, which are partly webbed.

They can also move quickly on land when necessary, lifting their bodies high off the ground. The Australian freshwater crocodile has been observed galloping, and muggers and caimans sometimes travel long distances on land if their home pools dry up.

▽ A mugger at the water's edge. To move swiftly on land, crocodiles lift their bodies clear of the ground on their powerful legs.

Birth and growing up

Crocodilians lay from about 12 to 100 eggs or more. They either bury them in the ground or make a kind of nest with soil and decaying plant matter. They guard them until hatched, in about two or three months.

The mother carries her young to a safe nursery in water along the shoreline. She watches over them for up to six months to a year, until they can take care of themselves.

△ It's hatching time, and an American alligator wriggles out of its shell. When they are ready to hatch, the baby alligators call out to their mother with a kind of quacking or croaking sound, and she opens up the nest.

▷ A baby crocodile takes a ride on its mother's head.

▽ Baby alligators lie on the bank with their tails in the water, just like their mother. Baby alligators often have yellow markings, but these fade as they grow older.

How crocodilians live

Crocodilians are often found in large groups. They live peacably together, although the males often fight and bellow at each other during the mating season.

△ Alligators usually live together in harmony, sharing the same stretch of water.

The females defend their nests with some ferocity. Like man, crocodilians are the masters of their environment. But their eggs are eaten by monitor lizards, some birds and monkeys, and raccoons. Wading birds also snatch the young.

△ An American
alligator with a leg
missing, lost in a fight
with another male
during the mating
season.

▷ A female alligator
looks suitably ferocious
as she defends her nest.

Crocodilians spend most of their day lying on the riverbank basking. They become active in the early evening, when it is time to hunt their prey.

When young, most crocodilians feed on insects and other small animals that live in and around the water. As they grow up, they begin to eat larger animals, such as fish and frogs. Later they feed on large birds and mammals.

▽ It is not easy to see this mugger hidden among the lotus plants. Crocodilians often lie in wait for animals who come down to the water to drink.

Crocodilians can replace their teeth over and over again. Their sharp teeth are more suited to holding prey than cutting it up. With large prey, they usually grab hold and roll and thrash about until a chunk of flesh is detached.

The muscles that close the jaws are very strong, enabling them to drag animals into the water. But the muscles that open their jaws are weak, allowing a strong person to hold a crocodile's mouth shut.

△ A crocodile savors an impala antelope, which it has dragged down to the bottom. Crocodilians can tear a large animal to pieces by violent twisting movements with their tearing teeth.

△ Fish hurtle through the air in all directions as a mugger lunges.

▷ An alligator settles down to enjoy a meal of fish.

▷ Reptile eats reptile as a mugger devours a snake.

▽ An alligator has caught an unwary raccoon, which it proceeds to swallow.

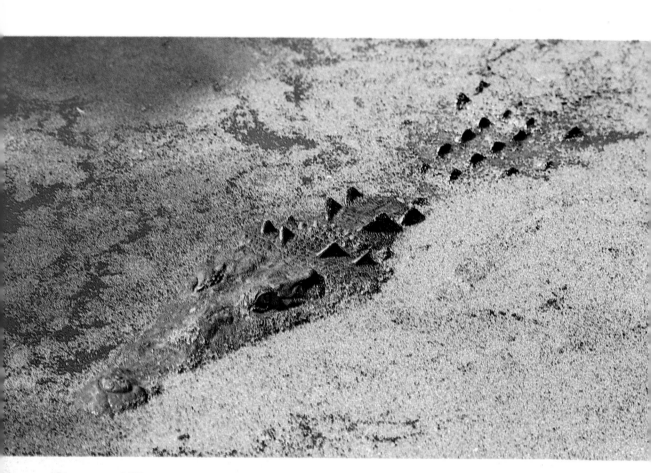

Crocodilians use stealth and camouflage to catch their prey. They can blend in with their surroundings very easily and have the patience to wait until suitable prey comes along. They can also move silently through the water.

Alligators usually hibernate in winter, digging dens in muddy banks.

△ A crocodile moves quietly and stealthily through the water, almost submerged under the algae covered surface.

▷ A wading bird appears unconcerned by the presence of crocodiles, which look not unlike the half submerged branch it is perching on.

▽ A crocodile crawls out of the water onto the nest of a lily-trotter, a bird of the swamps

Saving the crocodile

Many species of crocodilian are in need of protection. Hunters have killed them by the thousands for their skins, used in making such products as pocketbooks, shoes and belts.

Crocodile farms have been set up to breed some species. Young adults are released in habitats where they had been hunted out of existence. But the aim is partly to make hunting possible again.

▽ Newly hatched young scuttle around on an alligator farm in Florida.

△ A keeper holds a
baby crocodile on a
crocodile farm in
Zimbabwe.

◁ On this crocodile
farm in Thailand, the
animals are bred for
their skins.

The story of crocodilians

△ When you look at an alligator's leg and foot, it is easy to see links with the dinosaurs of prehistoric times.

The ruling reptiles

About 200 million years ago, a group of awesome reptiles began to rule the earth. They included all the great lumbering dinosaurs and they reigned supreme for 130 million years. The crocodilians of today are the only remaining members of that group, and they have changed very little over the 70 million years since mammals began to dominate the animal kingdom.

The crocodile in ancient times

People have always been fascinated by crocodilians, with their powerful, snapping jaws and their stealthy, monster-like appearance. The ancient Egyptians worshiped the Nile crocodile thousands of years ago as a symbol of the water god who caused the River Nile to rise every year and bring fertility to the land. Later, the crocodile became a symbol of the Egyptian god of evil. It is also thought that the leviathan, a monstrous creature featured in the Book of Job, in the Bible, was a crocodile.

Not much difference

There are only minor differences between crocodiles and alligators, and all the different species are thought of as crocodilians. The different names arose from two groups of settlers centuries apart, and both came from words meaning "lizard."

The word "crocodile" comes from the Latin "crocodilus," the name which the ancient Romans gave to the animals when the Roman Empire spread into

△ An alligator swims by another reptile – a turtle – that has also changed little since reptiles ruled the world.

△ The Nile crocodile was often depicted by artists of ancient Egypt, more than 4,000 years ago.

northern Africa 2,000 years ago. The word "alligator" comes from the Spanish "el lagarto," used by the first Spanish settlers in North America over 400 years ago.

Protection and survival

The hunting of crocodiles and alligators around the world for their skins has seriously endangered most species. The destruction of their natural habitats has also had a serious effect on the number of crocodilians left in the world.

Legal protection of the American alligator has helped its recovery in the United States. In India, special sanctuaries created for the gharial, which 15 years ago had almost become extinct, have revived its chances of survival. But despite the banning of the trade in skins, many other species have come close to extinction. The chief problems are excessive hide hunting, poor enforcement of the law and loss of habitat.

It is usually only when a species of animal is reduced or wiped out that we realize how the balance of nature has been upset. It often leads to the increase in numbers of other creatures, sometimes with unpleasant effects on the people of the area.

△ In some states laws protecting the alligator have led to its recovery, and now a certain amount of trading in alligator leather is permitted again.

Facts and records

Oldest

Little is known about how long crocodilians survive in the wild. But the greatest recorded age for a crocodilian in captivity is over 70 years. Ages of up to a hundred have been claimed, but never satisfactorily proved.

△ A young American alligator, if it survives into adulthood and then escapes the hunter's gun, can expect to live to a ripe old age.

Largest

Reports of the size of crocodilians have been greatly exaggerated. Crocodilians continue to grow for most of their life, but large specimens are becoming rarer as older animals in the wild are being killed off. The estuarine, or saltwater, crocodile is regarded as the largest of all reptiles. The adult male averages about 4.6 m (15 ft) in length, and occasional specimens reach 6 m (20 ft). In the past there have been reports of monsters as long as 10 m (33 ft).

△ Estuarines on a crocodile farm in Malaysia. This species grows into the largest of the crocodilians and has a reputation as a maneater.

Maneaters

The estuarine crocodile also has the reputation for being the most feared "maneater" of all the crocodilians. Hundreds of Japanese soldiers are said to have been attacked and killed by estuarines one night in February 1945. The men were trapped in a swamp on an island in the Bay of Bengal, some already dead and many wounded. Attracted by the blood and the noise of battle, the crocodiles moved in from miles around. Only about 20 men survived.

Glossary

Algae
Simple plants often found on the surface of stagnant water.

Balance of nature
The manner in which all living things react with each other and with the world they live in. If a species of animal or plant is reduced or wiped out, it can have a marked effect on other living things, especially those that feed on it or are eaten by it.

Caimans
Some species of crocodilian, very closely related to alligators, that are found in Central and South America.

Environment
The surroundings, or habitat, in which an animal lives.

Extinction
The state of having died out completely, without a living member of the species surviving on earth.

Farm
A place where crocodiles are raised. The eggs are carefully looked after and hatched in incubators—containers kept at the right temperature.

Gharial
A crocodilian that lives in India and has a long, slender snout.

Habitat
The natural surroundings in the wild where a particular species lives.

Hibernate
To go into a special, deep sleep throughout the winter, as some animals do.

Maneater
A name often applied to some of the more ferocious crocodilians that might attack and even eat people.

Sanctuary
A protected area, where a particular species is protected, looked after and given every opportunity to breed.

Species
A special kind of animal or plant. Animals and plants of the same species produce young of that species.

Index